EDGAR'S WALKING GUIDES

CHARLIE CHAPLIN'S LONDON

Copyright © Edgar's Guides Ltd, 2020

All rights reserved. No part of this book may be reprinted or reproduced or utilised in any form or by any electronic, mechanical or other means, now known or hereafter invented, including photocopying and recording, or in any information storage or retrieval system, without the prior permission in writing of the publishers.

All images publisher's own unless stated. Contemporary newspaper illustrations courtesy the British Library Board.

ISBN 978-1-8382342-4-9

Published by Edgar's Guides Ltd
71-75 Shelton Street, London WC2H 9JQ

Peruse the full catalogue,
access video clips and download free extras at
www.EdgarsGuides.com

No. 5

CHARLIE CHAPLIN'S LONDON

EDGAR SAYS

"There's something utterly thrilling about conducting one's own tour of history as you perambulate the thoroughfares, away from the crowds, able to pause on a whim to savour the moment. Allow me to be your companion as I guide you to some of my favourite places, from the well-known to the obscure, and suggest some of my preferred establishments for refreshment along the way. My thanks to my chums Mr. Richard Jones and Mr. Adam Wood for mapping out this excursion."

SAFETY NOTICE

Please be sure to be careful as you walk the route. Stay familiar with your surroundings at all times, and take particular care when you are crossing roads. Every effort has been made to ensure that the directions are accurate, but obviously, things can change and mistakes can be made, so the publishers cannot be held responsible for errors or their consequences. In the current Covid-aware times there are sanitising pots at Underground stations, which we recommend using before setting out. Please also be aware that some parts of the route may require the wearing of face masks, so ensure you have one with you at all times. Other than that, enjoy the walk and I hope it brings you as much joy as it did me when I encountered the wonderful places that you will be visiting.

CHARLIE CHAPLIN'S LONDON

Start: Elephant and Castle Underground Station (Bakerloo and Northern Lines)

End: The Three Stags public house
67 Kennington Road, London SE1 7PZ
Telephone to reserve 'Chaplin's Corner': 020 7928 5974

Duration: 4 hours
(add 30 minutes if walking Chaplin-style)

Best of Times: Any time, but as several stops are pubs we suggest afternoons and evenings

Charlie Chaplin. The mere mention of the name instantly conjures up the image of a small man, wearing oversized, baggy trousers and tight black jacket, and sporting a hat, cane and toothbrush moustache.

Chaplin was the world's first film star, becoming incredibly popular as silent movies exploded in the early twentieth century, his comedy short films making him a millionaire almost overnight. But before landing in America and entering the burgeoning film industry,

Chaplin had spent his early years in poverty-stricken South London, brought up by a mother struggling with mental illness, his father almost entirely absent from his young son's life.

In September 1921, Charlie Chaplin came home. It was the year that perhaps his most famous film – *The Kid* – was released, the first movie Chaplin had made which added drama to his usual brand of slapstick comedy, and his first to run over an hour. He was, at this point, the most famous movie star in the world, Hollywood's favourite comedian. Four years earlier he had signed a contract with First National to produce eight films, for which he would receive an astronomical one million dollars – the equivalent of $24,000,000 today.

Between 1914 and 1967 Chaplin would make eighty-two films, the vast majority in the silent era, and such was his popularity that he released two – *City Lights* and *Modern Times* – without dialogue to great acclaim, despite the fact that sound had been used in filmmaking for several years. The first film in which Chaplin spoke was 1940's *The Great Dictator*, a political satire on the threat of Hitler's Nazi ideal. A total of sixty-four featured him in his most famous role, a good-hearted down-at-heel vagrant known as the Tramp.

In 1972 Chaplin received an Honorary Oscar, and he was knighted in 1975, two years before his death at the age of 88.

But in September 1921, at the height of his worldwide fame, Charlie Chaplin came home to visit the haunts of his boyhood in South London.

It was a childhood as far removed from his life in America as could be imagined.

In the late Victorian era, unless you happened to be born into a family of relatively comfortable means, life in the capital was one of struggle. And neither of Chaplin's parents could claim such as position.

His mother, Hannah Harriet Pedlingham Hill, was born on 6th August 1865 at 11 Camden Street, Walworth, south of the Thames. Both her parents had been married before. Mrs Hill was a widow as a result of the accidental death of her first husband Henry Hodges; this meant an older half-brother, Harry, for Hannah, and a sister Kate was born five years later.

Walworth was a bustling, hard-working, tight-knit community and, like many in their position, the Hill family moved with regularity from room to room, taking lodgings where they could. By 1885 they were living at 57 Brandon Street, the home of Mrs Hill's former brother-in-law, Joseph Hodges. It was on 16th March that year that a 19-year-old Hannah gave birth to a son, who she named Sidney John Hill.* Although no father was named on the baptismal record, the infant would not be long without one.

On 22nd June 1885, just fourteen weeks after Sydney's birth, Hannah married Charles Spencer Chaplin at St John's, Walworth.

Born on 18th March 1863 at 22 Orcus Street, Marylebone in North London, the fifth child of Spencer and Ellen, Chaplin had made his way south by the time of the marriage, for the wedding certificate records him as also living at 57 Brandon Street. The document also shows his stated occupation of 'Professional singer', although this may be more a case of ambition, for there is no surviving record of Charles Chaplin performing on any stage until 1887, but his new wife, Hannah, is listed in a number of bookings starting in 1884.

Like many young people of the time, the great era of the music hall, the lure of the limelight attracted

---

* Although his name is recorded this way on the baptism register, throughout his life Sydney himself spelt his name with a 'Y', and it is this style we have used throughout this book.

both Charles and Hannah. In 1886, more than two hundred venues across the country offered weekly entertainment – 36 in London alone – and all needed performers to fill the bill. Many of the London-based entertainers resided south of the Thames, in areas such as Kennington and Brixton, and local taverns such as the Horns, the Tankard and the Three Stags became the background for their magnificent Sunday morning promenading. All would feature in the life of the young Charlie Chaplin, as you will hear.

As 'Lily Harley', Hannah appeared in May 1884 at the Bijou Music Hall on the Blackfriars Road, and in November at the Castle on Camberwell Road. She engaged an agent, whose placements in *The Era*, the definitive entertainment periodical, described her as "that charming little chanter" and reported appearances in Dublin, Belfast and Glasgow. One listing for 7th May 1886 records her as appearing at the South London Palace, Lambeth, on a billed topped by Vesta Tilley and featuring one of the earliest appearances by a 16 year old Marie Lloyd.

Charles Chaplin's career was slower to get started, but following his appearance at the Folly Variety Theatre in Manchester in June 1887 – with his wife Hannah appearing on the same bill – his engagements increased dramatically.

It was into this background of entertainment that Charles Spencer Chaplin Jr was born in Walworth in 1889. As if to underline the everyday nature of the event, his parents failed to register the birth, but Chaplin himself believed he was born on 16th April, 1889, at East Street, a stone's throw from Brandon Street, where Sydney had been born, and Camden Street, where his parents also lived for a short time.

At the time father Charles was performing at Hull on a week-long engagement, and the bookings continued. The following year, five of his most popular songs were released by music publishers – a clear indication of his growing success. As a result, the family were able to move into rooms at the much smarter West Square, and for a while lived a comfortable existence.

But Charles Chaplin's very popularity brought its own problems, as it did for many music hall performers, as they were expected to mingle with the audiences at the bars of the venue where they were appearing to encourage spending. The result was that Chaplin Sr, like so many of his contemporaries, succumbed to alcoholism, and this would feature heavily in his son's memories of his early days.

But for now, the illness had yet to affect his performances, and Chaplin Sr was booked for a three-month tour of America commencing in August 1890.

On his return, or soon after, his relationship with Hannah ended. But she would not be on her own for long; in the autumn of 1891 she formed a short-lived relationship with another music hall star, George Dryden Wheeler, whose star was at the time in the ascendancy thanks to the song *The Miner's Dream of Home*, which he performed under the stage name Leo Dryden.

On 31st August 1892 a child, George Dryden Wheeler Jr, was born. For six months Hannah raised her three young sons, until suddenly, in the spring of 1893, Wheeler Sr turned up at her lodgings and removed his son, possibly as a result of Hannah beginning to show signs of the mental fragility which would afflict her in the years ahead.

It was not until Charlie Chaplin became a huge star that Wheeler Sr told his son the truth of his birth, at which point the younger half-brother, starting out on a career in vaudeville, wrote to Charlie and Sydney in Hollywood. After two years the elder brothers finally accepted him; Wheeler was reunited with them and Hannah in America, and would work for Chaplin Studios. He appeared in small roles in Charlie's final two films, *Monsieur Verdoux* and *Limelight*. His father, Leo Dryden, continued his career until the decline of the music hall in the 1930s, at which point he took to busking in the streets.

Leo Dryden in later life
Source gallica.bnf.fr / Bibliothèque nationale de France

Following the removal of her youngest son from her life, and with it financial support from Leo Dryden, Hannah, Sydney and Charlie descended into a precarious existence due to financial instability.

With payments from Charles Sr being irregular at best, and Hannah unable to find work on the stage, she began taking in needlework in order to provide a roof over their heads, and food – such as it was – on the table.

One winter it became apparent that the boys needed new clothes, but without the money to buy them Hannah resorted to re-purposing some of her own with the help of her sewing machine. An old jacket, with red and black striped sleeves and pleated shoulders, was turned into a new coat for Sydney, who wept at the thought of what his schoolfriends would say; he was henceforth known as 'Joseph and his coat of many colours'. Charlie, sporting a pair of his mother's red tights cut down to produce stockings with a pleated appearance, was 'Sir Francis Drake.'

In his autobiography Chaplin recalled the family moving from room to room, his mother hunched over her sewing machine, desperately trying to make ends meet. Eventually Charles Sr's weekly payments of 10s stopped completely. He had, by this time, entered into a relationship with a young woman known only today as 'Louise', and they'd had a son in 1894 – another half-brother for Chaplin. As a consequence installment payments on the sewing machine mounted, and it was soon taken away. A solicitor, seeing no financial gain in the case for himself, advised Hannah to throw herself at the mercy of the Lambeth authorities, in the hope that they might succeed in forcing Chaplin Sr to support his family.

There was no alternative; Hannah, Sydney and Charlie were forced to present themselves at the Lambeth Workhouse, on Renfrew Road. The boys were swiftly sent to Norwood Schools, at Hanwell in

West London, which served to educate the children of Lambeth's poorer families.

Chaplin later recalled:

"Although at Hanwell we were well looked after, it was a forlorn existence. Sadness was in the air; it was in those country lanes through which we walked, a hundred of us two abreast. How I disliked those walks, and the villages through which we passed, the locals staring at us! We were known as inmates of the 'booby hatch', a slang term for the workhouse."

Chaplin at Norwood Schools

After a brief respite, when Hannah concocted a ruse for the three of them to be reunited for a wonderful day spent at Kennington Park, Charlie and Sydney were carted off again to Hanwell – quite literally, in a baker's van. This time, there was to be no happy reunion. Hannah was taken to Lambeth Infirmary with signs of mental illness, and then transferred to Cane Hill Asylum.

As Lambeth Borough authorities had finally traced Charles Chaplin Sr to a house on Kennington Road, the boys were discharged into his care, being driven the twelve miles from Hanwell in the same baker's van. By this time their father's drinking had taken its grim hold, and the six weeks they spent with Charles Sr and Louise, remembered by Charlie as a living hell, ended when Hannah was discharged and arrived to save them.

But two incidents from this period left their mark on Charlie Chaplin. His father recommended him to an acquaintance living nearby, William Jackson, who was the founder of a popular clog-dancing troupe called the Eight Lancashire Lads. Charlie was taken on and toured with the troupe to great affection from audiences, thereby gaining his first experience of working the boards. He performed with the Lads at a benefit concert put on for his father, who was very ill, later remembering "The night of the benefit my father appeared on the stage breathing with difficultly, and with painful effort made a speech. I stood at the side of the stage watching him, not realising that he was a dying man."

Charles Chaplin Sr would pass away less than a year later, aged just thirty seven.

It was during his time with the Lancashire Lads that Chaplin planted the seed of an idea which would reap great dividends in the future. Aware that clog dancing was not the limit of his ambition, Chaplin wanted to be a boy comedian, and had the idea of a double act with another of the Lads, calling themselves 'Bristol and Chaplin, the Millionaire Tramps'. An act was developed which would see the boys dressed as tramps but wearing big diamond rings, enacting various comedy sketches based on the contradiction. Sadly, the material never saw the light of day, but the idea of a comedic tramp would provide his fortune.

Another facet of the character was discovered and developed after Chaplin saw a local character, known to posterity as 'Rummy Binks', outside the Queen's Head pub, where his uncle Spencer Chaplin was the manager. With his father treating the pub as a second home, it was no surprise that his son would hang around the area and it was there that he observed Rummy's shuffling walk, which he imitated and, seeing that it always guaranteed laughter, incorporated it into his future act.

As Charlie took his first tentative steps into the entertainment world, his mother's mental health was declining. Sydney had decided on a career at sea, and had left the country aboard SS *Exmouth* and then the SS *Norman*, employed as assistant steward.

Hannah and Charlie moved from room to room, making money anyway they could, with the young Chaplin spending an increasing amount of time with his friend Wally McCarthy, the son of a friend of Hannah's from her music hall days. One afternoon Charlie returned home to be told by the neighbours that his mother had 'gone mad'; he discovered it was indeed the case, and led her to the Lambeth Infirmary, from where she was transferred again to Cane Hill Asylum, recorded as 'insane'. She remained there for eight months, but on discharge was not fully cured – throughout her life Hannah would suffer mental illness, but after Charlie and Sydney brought her over to live with them in California in 1921 she enjoyed a very peaceful seven years, before her death in August 1928.

*

Charlie Chaplin's route to fame and fortune in Hollywood came as a result of him being engaged by the theatre impresario Fred Karno, who took his troupe on an American tour first in September 1910 – on which another member of the troupe was Stan Laurel – and then October 1912. During this second trip Chaplin was scouted for the burgeoning movie industry, and signed to the Keystone Film Company. Other early film stars who enjoy early success with Keystone include Harold Lloyd, Roscoe 'Fatty' Arbuckle and Gloria Swanson. By the end of 1914 Chaplin was one of the biggest names in Hollywood, and, thanks to his screen persona the Little Tramp, one of its most famous faces too.

*

There are many books on the life of Charlie Chaplin, but to hear his own recollections of his boyhood we recommend his own memoir, *My Autobiography* (1964). For a full, detailed account of Chaplin's life and work, see David Robinson's excellent *Chaplin: His Life and Art* (2001 edition).

During this tour of Charlie Chaplin's London, you will visit many of the places mentioned above and much more.

The tour is a full four hours, so if you intend walking

it in one go you'll be pleased to hear that there are a number of places associated with Chaplin where you can revive yourself with a refreshment.

The mid-point is the Dog House public house (stop 20), and the Queen's Head, now a café (stop 23), is two-thirds of the way round. The tour of Charlie Chaplin's London ends at the Three Stags. All three establishments were known to the future film star.

We also pass close to Kennington and Oval Underground stations, should you wish to finish the walk early and return at a later date to complete it.

As you walk along the thoroughfares of Walworth, Kennington and Lambeth, keep an eye open for appearances from South London's most famous son. The locals are very proud of him, quite rightly so, and his image appears on murals, framed prints in coffee shops, and sometimes their menus.

Enjoy your tour of cinematic history, and, as you sit with a well-earned refreshment at our journey's end at the Three Stag's pub, take a moment to dwell on the journey taken by a poverty-stricken, semi-literate small boy from the mean streets who made his way to the glitz and glamour of Hollywood through his ability to make people smile.

Charlie Chaplin's London

Edgar's Guide To...

CHARLIE CHAPLIN TIMELINE

1863	Charles Chaplin Sr born at Marylebone on 18th March.
1865	Hannah Hill born at Walworth on 6th August.
1885	Sidney John Hill born to Hannah on 16th March; baptised at St John's Church, Walworth on 1st April.
1885	Charles Chaplin and Hannah Hill marry at St John's on 22nd June.
1889	Son Charles Spencer Chaplin born on 16th April at East Street, Walworth.
1889	The family move to West Square, Kennington.
1890	Charles Chaplin Sr engaged on a tour of America from August to October.
c1890	Charles and Hannah Chaplin separate.
1892	Leo Wheeler Dryden born to Hannah Chaplin and Leo Dryden Sr on 31st August.
1893	Leo Dryden Sr leaves Hannah, taking his son.

1894	Birth of a son, name unknown, to Charles Chaplin Sr and a woman named Louise.
1898	Hannah, Sydney and Charlie admitted to Lambeth Workhouse on 22nd July from Farmer's Road, Kennington.
1898	Charlie and Sydney transferred to Norwood Schools, Hanwell on 30th July.
1898	Charlie and Sydney returned to Lambeth Workhouse on 12th August, and are discharged with Hannah. They spend a few hours in Kennington Park before returning to the workhouse later that same day.
1898	Hannah admitted to Lambeth Infirmary on 6th September, and transferred nine days later to Cane Hill Asylum.
1898	Charlie and Sydney discharged into the care of their father on 27th September. They live with him and Louise at 287 Kennington Road.
1898	Hannah discharged from Cane Hill Asylum on 12th November and collects Charlie and Sydney. They move to a room in Methley Street.

1898	Charlie joins the Eight Lancashire Lads, performing with them in Manchester on 26th December.
1901	Charlie sees his father for the last time, at the Three Stags public house. Charles Sr is admitted to St Thomas's Hospital on 29th April, and dies on 9th May aged just 38.
1903	Hannah admitted to Lambeth Infirmary on 5th May, and committed to Cane Hill Asylum as a lunatic six days later.
1903	Charlie plays his first dramatic role as 'Sam' in *Jim, A Romance of Cockayne* at Kingston.
1903	Charlie plays 'Billy' in the play *Sherlock Holmes*, subsequently joining the company on tour. Sydney later joins the cast.
1904	Hannah discharged from Cane Hill Asylum on 2nd January and joins her sons on tour.
1905	Hannah admitted to Lambeth Infirmary on 6th March, and transferred to Cane Hill Asylum as a lunatic ten days later. She remains there until 1912.
1906	*Sherlock Holmes* play ends after four tours.
1907	Sydney Chaplin signs contract with Fred Karno troupe on 9th July, tours America.

1908	Charlie Chaplin signs contract with Karno on 21st February.
1908	Charlie and Sydney rent a flat at Glenshaw Mansions for when they are between tours.
1910	Charlie embarks on US tour with Karno troupe.
1912	Charlie returns to London in June to discover that Sydney has let the Glenshaw Mansions flat go.
1912	Charlie tours France and the Channel Islands with the Karno troupe during July and August.
1912	Charlie embarks on second US tour with Karno, departing on 2nd October. He doesn't return to England until 1921.
1913	Charlie signs a contract to join the Keystone Film Company on 16th December.
1914	His first film, *Making a Living*, is released on 2nd February, the first of 35 pictures he stars in that year.
1917	Signs contract on 17th June earning him a salary of $1,075,000 per year.
1921	Charlie returns to London and visits his boyhood haunts.

HIGHLIGHTS OF THE CHAPLIN'S LONDON WALK

Here are some of the thought-provoking highlights you will encounter as you make your way through the back streets and main thoroughfares of Charlie Chaplin's London:

- The bustling street on which Chaplin was born.
- The tucked-away church where his parents were married.
- The workhouse where Chaplin's mother was forced to take herself and her sons.
- The infirmary where Mrs Chaplin was admitted through mental illness.
- The public house where Chaplin saw the man whose walk inspired his greatest comic invention.
- The "little haven" that Chaplin and his brother kept for four years.
- The spot where Chaplin waited for a date with the first girl he ever loved.

Edgar's Guide To...

- The house where Chaplin and his brother lived with their father for an unhappy three months.
- The spot where Chaplin sat and, in the midst of his darkest despair, heard music which lifted his soul.
- The majestic building where Chaplin played with his closest childhood friend.
- The pub where Chaplin saw his father for the last time, and shared their one and only heartfelt moment.

And, as you wind your way around these fascinating locations, you will uncover buildings, pubs, streets and houses that have hardly changed since Chaplin's time, giving you a true sense of the movie star's earliest days and the London he knew.

To begin, head to Elephant & Castle Underground station, on the Northern and Bakerloo lines. Leave the station via the Shopping Centre Exit and turn immediately left onto the very busy Newington Butts, follow the curve of the station on your left. Within a few seconds you'll pass the site of what was the Elephant and Castle Shopping Centre on your left, opened in 1965 as one of Europe's first American-style indoor shopping malls, comprising 115 retailers over three storeys. Continue for a few steps and pause after the bus stop marked P to look across the road at the yellow-brick

....

1. METROPOLITAN TABERNACLE

Formed in 1650 at a time when Parliament had banned Baptist meetings, a small congregation braved prosecution by meeting at a Kennington house owned by a woman known to history only as the Widow Colfe. The Tabernacle Fellowship's first chapel was built near what is now the Tower Bridge area following the legalisation of the religion in 1688, and by the 1850s, when the famous Charles Haddon Spurgeon became pastor, the Fellowship met at nearby Royal Surrey Gardens Music Hall (of which more later), which provided seating for up to 10,000 worshippers.

The Metropolitan Tabernacle building opposite was originally opened in 1861 with a 6,000-seat auditorium. Within twenty years the church enjoyed a membership of 5,500 worshippers.

When the building burned down in 1898 the front portico and basement survived, and the church was rebuilt. It was struck by an incendiary bomb in May 1941, with the portico once again miraculously escaping unscathed. The Metropolitan Tabernacle

Charles Haddon Spurgeon, Pastor at the Metropolitan Tabernacle between 1861 and 1892

was rebuilt to a different design in 1957, retaining the frontage.

Continue walking along, following the pavement as it curves to the left after the traffic lights. Go past the trees and the bus stop marked R, then walk under the railway bridge and cross the entry road to the Elephant and Castle railway station. You are now walking south along the Walworth Road. Keep to the left side. Continue past the small wildflower meadow with the statue of an elephant, cross the office building slip road, and then over Heygate Street. Pass on your left the new Heritage Centre and Library, then enter the serene Walworth Square which contains a modern war memorial by sculptor Kenny Hunter. From this vantage point you are afforded a splendid view of the red-bricked building, which was

2. WALWORTH TOWN HALL

Built for the Vestry Board of St Mary, Newington, the building was officially opened on 8th August 1865, initially as the Vestry Hall, but was renamed Southwark Town Hall in 1900 when it became the headquarters of the Metropolitan Borough of Southwark.

Newington Public Library, now the Newington Art Academy, was built in 1892, and the narrow building connecting the two was added in 1893.

Vestry Hall, Walworth c1890. Courtesy English Heritage

When the London Borough of Southwark was created in 1965 the council headquarters were relocated, and the building was renamed Walworth Town Hall, continuing to host council functions such as serving as the area's Registry Office.

In 2006 the Cuming Museum, which had been open to visitors on galleries on the first floor of the Library next door since 1906, moved into the Hall. Local resident Richard Cuming (1777–1870) began his collection at a very young age with some fossils and a coin given to him by a friend.

A lifetime's collection of objects from the local area and further afield passed to his son, Henry Syer Cuming (1817-1902), who added his own items before bequeathing the entire Cuming collection to the people of Southwark. Between them they had acquired all kinds of objects from around the world, from tickets and toys from local fairs to clothing worn by North American Inuit people and examples of early taxidermy from Europe.

A fire in March 2013 badly damaged the roof, forcing the Museum to close. The Cuming collection was rehoused at its newly-built home, the Southwark Heritage Centre you passed a few moments ago.

Redevelopment plans for the Grade II-listed Walworth Town Hall, intended to convert the building to a community hub, were submitted in June 2020 but work has been paused during the Covid pandemic.

....

Leave Walworth Square to resume walking along Walworth Road, pausing on the corner to look over the road at the grand Georgian building with the word 'Manor' above the portico. This refers to its current use as the Manor of Walworth pub and budget hotel, but the building is named John Smith House after the former Leader of the Labour Party, who had their headquarters here between 1980 and 1997. Built between 1793-99 as Walworth Terrace, it originally comprised twelve houses, including, ironically, at one point the home to the Walworth Conservative Club, but five were destroyed during WWII.

Turn left to resume walking down Walworth Road and examine the frontages of the Town Hall and Library as you pass. To the right of the Art Academy, on the corner of Larcom Street, is

3. THE WALWORTH CLINIC

Designed by Borough architect Percy Smart, the foundation stone to what was the Public Health Centre at Southwark was laid on 11th July 1936, with the building officially opening on 25th September 1937. One of a number of pioneering health centres built at the end of the 1930s, the Centre brought all the borough's health services under one roof, predating this stipulation set in the National Health Services Act of 1946 by a decade.

A plaque above the door features the quotation 'The Health of the People is the Highest Law', translated from the Roman statesman Cicero, and at the top of the façade is a sculpture featuring a mother and three children, symbolising the focus of the Centre.

The building was awarded Grade II status in 2010.

Walworth Road c1890

Today the front part contains an NHS Sexual Health clinic, while separate office accommodation occupies the rear.

....

Turn left into Larcom Street, keeping to the left-hand side, and take a moment to look up at the corner of the Walworth Clinic at the blue plaque to the 'father of computing', Charles Babbage, who is believed to have been born nearby at 44 Crosby Row, off the Walworth Road, in 1791. Continue walking along Larcom Street, and alongside the entrance to Larcom House note the blue plaque to Michael Faraday, discoverer of electromagnetism, who was born on Newington Butts also in 1791. Cross Ethel Street and continue to the end of Larcom Street, past St John's CoE Primary School, then look over to the right at

4. ST JOHN'S CHURCH

Charlie Chaplin's elder half-brother Sydney was baptised here on 1st April 1885 as 'Sidney John Hill' – his mother's maiden name – with the parents recorded as Hannah Harriet Hill, mother, but no father named. Her address was given as 57 Brandon Street. Sydney had been born on 16th March, when Hannah was not yet twenty years old. The identity of his father has never been established, although Hannah later told her sons a fanciful tale of eloping to South Africa with a rich middle-aged bookmaker named Hawkes, returning alone with a child on the way.

Just three months after Sydney's birth, on 22nd June, Hannah married 22-year-old Charles Chaplin here at St John's, witnessed by one George Bailey and Hannah's mother, Mary Ann Hill. Both bride and groom gave their address as 57 Brandon Street.

The Anglican St John the Evangelist Church was built in 1859/60 by Henry Jarvis, the District Surveyor.

Charles Chaplin

Edgar's Guide To...

Hannah Chaplin

A footpath to the left of the perimeter fence allows you to wander around the church for a closer look, and it is well worth taking the time to do so. Return back to this corner, then continue along Larcom Street and follow it as it turns to the right. We have left behind the hustle and bustle of modern life, and are now deep into the Walworth of Chaplin's time. The terraced houses here and around this area would have been familiar to the future comic genius.

Follow Larcom Street as it dog-legs first right and then left. The unusual shape of the street is a result of it being built in 1876, with the church grounds and school along with other gardens in the immediate area being already in place, so the street was built around them. On the right-hand side, just before you reach the end of the road, is the St John Centre, opened in 1900 under the auspices of the Rev A.W. Jephson, vicar of the church, as a community centre – a function it continues to provide today. High above the door, note the coat of arms bearing the Biblical inscription "Quit You Like Men".

At the end of the road turn left into Brandon Street. As you near the end of Brandon Street, before it curves to the left to become Wansey Street, cross over to the pedestrianised pathway between the two metal posts and follow this round to the right. Following the footpath round to the right, cross Rodney Road at the zebra crossing and stop by the Victory Primary School, which was previously known as

....

5. VICTORY PLACE SCHOOL

Named after the road which runs along its right-hand side, Victory Place School was opened on 24th November 1874, with a capacity of 1,000 children. It consisted of two separate buildings, one three storeys tall for the elder children (shown in the photograph opposite), and a single-storey building towards the rear of the site for infants. It was in this smaller class for the younger pupils that it is said a very young Charlie Chaplin was educated for a short time.

Although no records survive to confirm this, a former teacher named Mrs E.E. Turner-Dauncey is quoted in *Cinema Studies* (1960) as saying that she taught Chaplin at the school: "I remember his large eyes, his mass of dark curly hair, and his beautiful small hands. He was very sweet and so shy."

The school was rebuilt just before the Great War; all that survives of the original construction is the Gothic-styled building in the left-hand corner of the site, with the tall red chimneys, which is the caretaker's house.

Another local-born comic, Charlie Drake, attended Victory Place School in the 1930s.

Victory Place School

☞ *Return to Rodney Road and go over the zebra crossing. On the other side turn left, walking with the modern apartments on both left and right. After a few moments, at the corner of Larcom Street, you will see a pair of very large red-bricked buildings on the opposite side, which is the Walworth Peabody Estate, built in 1915. Cross Larcom Street, follow the exterior of the estate and, at the corner currently occupied by a wine bar called Diogenes the Dog, turn right into Wadding Street. Walk on the right side until you reach Content Street, then turn right.*

The yellow-bricked estate on your left with a tower and weather vane is Walters Close, sheltered accommodation built in 1961 by the Draper's Company to replace the old Newington Almshouses in Draper Street, which were demolished for road-widening at Elephant and Castle.

Walk to the end of Content Street, and take a moment at the end to admire the inner courts of the Peabody Estate now visible on your right. At the corner turn left, and when you get to the end of the road cross over to the modern brightly-coloured building and take a seat on the black-and-white seating, with your back to the red building. Look over at the corner you have just walked down, at the building with the overhanging first floor with its three white-framed windows, which is where, from the 1820s, stood the Duke of Suffolk (the same corner is shown opposite), named after Charles Brandon (1484-1545), the first Duke of Sussex. The pub was the venue for local inquests for over a century until its demolition in the late 1930s. Alongside stood

6. 57 BRANDON STREET

As we have heard, this was the address given by Hannah Hill when her son Sydney was baptised, and also by both Hannah and Charles Chaplin at the time of their marriage. On the wedding certificate the groom gave his profession as a 'Professional singer'.

At the time, 57 Brandon Street was owned by general dealer Joseph Hodges, the brother of Henry Hodges who had married Hannah's mother Mary Ann in 1854 but died after falling from an omnibus, leaving her a widow with a young son. Mary Ann married Charles

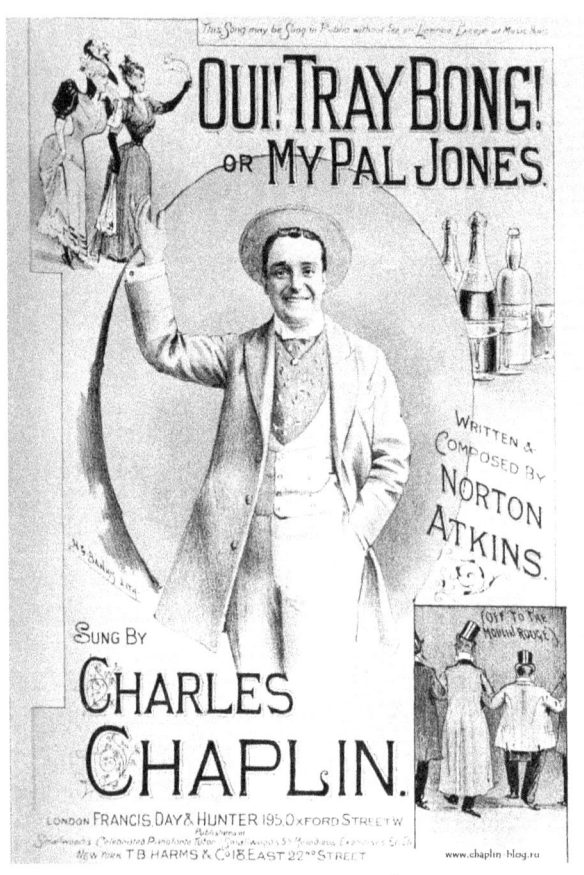

Sheet music cover, 1893

Hill in 1861, and the couple welcomed two daughters, Hannah (b1865) and Kate (b1870).

It is probable that Charles Chaplin rented a room in the house, leading to his meeting Hannah.

Walk right along Brandon Street, with the brightly-coloured modern buildings on your right, and immediately cross Charleston Street. Note the serene interior of Walters Court on your left as it comes into view. Continue along and take the next right into Browning Street. When safe, cross over to the left side. At the first corner cross over to pause at the black railings by the little green.

Look over at the road you have just crossed, which is Morecambe Street. Although virtually nothing survives of its past, this was previously known as

---

7. CAMDEN STREET

Chaplin's mother Hannah was born at No. 11 on 6th August 1865, to Charles and Mary Ann Hill. She was the first child born to the couple, joining Mary Ann's son from her first marriage, Henry Hodges. Another daughter, Kate, was born at nearby Bronti Place in January 1870.

In March 1890, following their marriage and the birth of son Charlie, Charles Sr and Hannah spent a short period living at No. 68 Camden Street.

....

The green space behind the railings is all that is left of the burial ground of York Street Congregational Chapel, which stood on this spot. A solitary tomb sits in the middle, remembering Richard Holbert and Captain James Wilson. The Chapel was built in 1790 and renamed Browning Hall in 1890 after the famous Victorian poet Robert Browning, who was baptised there in 1812. What was previously York Street was renamed Browning Street in 1937.

Continue walking along Browning Street, with the railings on your left. Pass the telephone box, then take the next left into King and Queen Street. Walk all the way to the end, noting as you go along on the right the affordable housing development (another Peabody Dwellings estate built in 1933), and on the left the wonderful Robert Browning Primary School, opened in 1883 as King and Queen Street School. Sydney Chaplin attended the school at the age of five, between March and May 1890, when his younger brother Charlie was just a year old, and the family lived at nearby 68 Camden Street.

Pause at the end of the road, on the corner of

Browning Hall, 1930s

8. EAST STREET

Although no official record exists of the time and place the future comedy genius Charles Spencer Chaplin first came into the world – it appears his parents never registered his birth – he himself stated he was born in East Street on 16th April 1889, and always celebrated that day as his birthday. At one point his grandfather Charles Hill, a shoemaker, had cheap premises on East Street – or East Lane, as it has always been known locally – so it is possible that his grandson was born there.

East Lane c1905

While street traders had sold their wares lining the Walworth Road for more than 200 years, it was only when construction work laying down tram lines began in 1875 that sellers were relocated to side streets East Lane, Westmoreland Street and Draper Street. Development works saw the markets in the latter two roads cease within a short number of years, and East Lane became the official site for the combined large market in 1880. Today it operates every day except Mondays.

It has been suggested that East Street was the inspiration for the title of Chaplin's 1917 film *Easy Street*.

Turn right into East Street and walk all the way to the end, enjoying the vibrant atmosphere of a busy market selling everything from shoes and handbags to fresh fruit and vegetables. The market is known for pickpockets, so take care with your personal possessions.

Pass under the suspended 'East Street Market' lettering at the end, and look up to your left, to see a blue plaque which commemorates Chaplin being born in the street.

Cross the busy Walworth Road via the traffic lights, veer right and then left into Penrose Street, which was once West Lane, a continuation of East Lane opposite; this crossroads formed the historic village centre of Walworth, and appears on maps as far back as 1681.

Continue walking along, under the railway bridge, passing the red-brick building on the left, which was the Walworth Postmen's Sorting Office, built in 1897. Take note of the villas on your left, including the doctor's surgery, which are relics of the area's Georgian past, and the later Victorian terrace on your right.

At the bottom, ignore the road as it turns left, and instead walk towards Sturgeon Road and the apparent dead-end and continue onto the pedestrianised path, past the school, and enter Pasley Park.

As you follow the path which cuts across the park diagonally to the right, towards the children's playground, pause by the information board on the right of the path and take a moment to contemplate that this relatively small area is all that remains of the massively popular

9. ROYAL SURREY GARDENS

Previously the grounds of Walworth Manor House, the 15 acre site was purchased in 1831 by the impresario Edward Cross as the location for the Royal Surrey Zoological Gardens, intended as competition for the London Zoo at Regent's Park which had been established three years earlier. Cross relocated animals from his menagerie at Exeter Exchange on the Strand, including giraffes, lions, tiger and a rhinoceros. More than 170 species were housed in cages contained within a 300ft circular domed glass conservatory, and attracted 8,000 visitors each day.

The gardens themselves were planted with exotic trees and plants, and picturesque pavilions erected, and a 3-acre lake for boating. From 1837 large public entertainments such as a re-enactment of the eruption of Mount Vesuvius were staged.

On Cross's death in 1854 the gardens were acquired by a company, who sold off the menagerie two years later to build Surrey Music Hall within the gardens, which boasted a capacity of 12,000 seated spectators, making it the largest venue in London.

For five years Surrey Music Hall was enormously popular, but was destroyed by fire in 1861. The gardens were eventually sold for redevelopment as residential property in 1877, and more than a century later, in the

Edward Cross painted in 1838

1980s, this small green space was opened between the housing developments.

Keep on the path with the children's play area on your left, then exit the park and cross over Manor Place, when safe to do so, then veer left on the other side, following the fence of Walworth Gardens as it curves right into what is Braganza Street.

We are now in Kennington. Pause outside the red-brick Territorial Army drill hall, on your right, which originates from a pair of houses built in 1833 and acquired by the 19th Surrey Rifle Volunteer Corps in 1865, before being enlarged in 1937. [Note: If for some reason you need to end the tour at this point, continue walking along Braganza Street, all the way to the end, and in a few minutes you'll come to Kennington Station (Northern line) on the corner.]

To continue the tour, with your back to the drill hall cross the road to walk down Doddington Grove, on the right-hand side. This road is lined on its left-hand side by local authority housing, built in the 1930s by Southwark Borough Council as part of their slum clearance scheme. Known as the Doddington Estate, the apartments are now in the main privately-owned, worth upwards of £300,000.

At the end, follow Doddington Grove as it bends to the right, then take the left turn into Doddington Place and walk with the green on your left. At the end turn right into Kennington Park Place, then cross over to take the first left into St Agnes Place, with its attractive row of Georgian houses on the left.

Keeping to the left side, cross Royal Road, and after a few moments pause on the corner of Kennington Park Gardens, which was formerly

---

10. FARMER'S ROAD

After Charles Sr and Hannah had parted, she, Sydney and Charlie rented a room at No. 10 in the summer of 1898, at a time when the family found themselves carrying their meagre possessions from lodging to lodging with alarming frequency. Chaplin later recalled, "We kept moving from one back-room to another; it was like a game of draughts."

It was from 10 Farmers Road that the family entered Lambeth Workhouse on 22nd July 1898. Sydney was thirteen years old, Charlie nine. After eight days the boys were transferred to authority-run Norwood Schools at Hanwell, West London for a fortnight, with Hannah remaining at the workhouse.

Farmer's Road was a row of cottages named after

Richard Farmer, who established the Farmer's Vitriol Makers factory here – sulphuric acid – in 1796. The company moved to other premises in the early 1870s and the site cleared, with the foundation stone for St Agnes Church being laid in 1874.

Before moving on, take a moment to admire St Agnes Church, originally a large place of worship designed by the renowned Victorian architect George Gilbert Scott Jr which could house 1,000 worshippers. This was destroyed during WWII and the current church opened in 1956.

Enter the park via the entrance on your right. Walk straight ahead, then turn left at the next path (with a Friends of Kennington Park noticeboard in front of a children's playground). With the playground on your left, follow the fence as it curves to the left. Continue straight on this path, passing the cafeteria on your left, and at the next fork follow the path to the right of the signpost. Pass the three benches on your left, then take the first path off to the left, walking towards a large ornamental bowl.

This is all that remains of the ornate Slade Fountain, based on a design exhibited at the Great Exhibition of 1851 and funded by local art collector Felix Slade.

Edgar's Guide To...

The Slade Fountain

A huge bronze vase depicting a scene from the Old Testament sat on top until it was stolen in the 1850s. There are several objects of historical importance within the park, including a lovely War Memorial. Should you have time, or intend to return on another occasion, *information can be found at www.kenningtonpark.org.*

Pass the bowl and continue along the same path you were on, with the white shelter and then railings on your left, and if possible take a seat on a vacant bench.

11. KENNINGTON PARK

Hannah Chaplin had been at Lambeth Workhouse for three weeks and had not seen her sons for a fortnight when she concocted a plan for the family to be reunited.

Telling the authorities she intended to discharge the three of them from their care, Charlie and Sydney were transferred back from Norwood Schools on 12th August 1898. They were met at the workhouse gates early that morning by their mother, who handed them their disinfected but unpressed clothes, and the crumpled trio made their way here to Kennington Park, where they spent the day creating memories of happier times with their mother which Charlie and Sydney would remember for the rest of their lives.

Sydney had managed to save ninepence from doing odd jobs, so they bought half a pound of black cherries, which the family ate while sitting on a park bench, possibly on this very spot. A sheet of newspaper was scrunched up into a ball, tied with string, and the

Kennington Park c1900

three of them played catch.

At lunchtime they went to a nearby coffee shop and spent the remainder of the money on a feast comprising a twopenny teacake, a penny bloater and two halfpenny cups of tea. Afterwards they returned to the park, with Sydney and Charlie resuming their game while Hannah sat nearby contentedly crocheting.

Eventually they made their way back to the workhouse, just before teatime, annoying the authorities because they had to go through the same admittance procedure. It was a Friday, so the family enjoyed the weekend together before the boys were sent away once again to Norwood Schools.

Hannah remained at the workhouse until 6th September, when, following worrying signs of mental ill-health, she was admitted to Lambeth Infirmary. Nine days later was transferred to Cane Hill Asylum, south of London, receiving treatment for two months.

During this time the boys were discharged into the care of their father, leaving Norwood Schools on 27th September.

Previously a much larger area known as Kennington Common, this space saw large crowds listen to public speakers including Methodists John Wesley and George Whitefield, who preached to 30,000 people in 1739, and an estimated 50,000 who heard an address by Chartist leader Feargus O'Connor in 1848. As a result of developments to the surrounding roads it opened as the smaller Kennington Park in 1854.

....

Resume walking along the path, straight ahead, then exit the park between the two red-brick columns. Once on the pavement turn left, then cross over the road via the traffic lights towards the large red-and-yellow-brick building. On the other side, walk along Brixton Road with this building on your left.

Today the Kennington Park office and studios complex,

General Cab Company, Brixton Road, c1910

the building was constructed in 1905 by the General Cab Company to house offices and three-storey garages for 2,000 motor vehicles, complete with repair shops and cab washing facilities. Some 1,500 taxis operated from this base daily in the early 20th century, exiting the black front gates on your left.

Continue walking along Brixton Road, go over Cranmer Road and then cross over to the right side of Brixton Road via the traffic lights. On the other side, turn left then cross over Handforth Road and then continue along Brixton Road, with the rows of Victorian apartments on your right.

Go over Crewdson Road, then South Island Place – which appears on old maps as South Highland Place, but as an indication of the Londoner's pronunciation appears to have lost the 'H' at some point – then pause at the tree to look up at the blue plaque marking

12. GLENSHAW MANSIONS

In 1908, with Charlie and Sydney both working for Fred Karno and bringing in good money, they decided to rent a flat for when they returned to London between tours of the provinces.

They took on No. 15 Glenshaw Mansions, and set about furnishing its four rooms with second-hand goods from a shop in nearby Newington Butts, including an upright piano which took them over their budget of £40.

Chaplin would later remember the brothers' haven: "We carpeted the front room and linoleumed the others and bought an upholstered suite – a couch and two armchairs. In one corner of the sitting-room we put a fretwork Moorish screen, lighted from behind by a coloured yellow bulb, and in the opposite corner, on a gilt easel, a pastel in a gilded frame. The picture was of a nude model standing on a pedestal, looking sideways over her shoulder as a bearded artist is about to brush a fly off her bottom. This objet d'art and the screen, I thought, made the room. The final décor was a combination of Moorish cigarette shop and a French whore-house. But we loved it."

The Chaplin brothers kept 15 Glenshaw Mansions for four years, with grandfather Charles Hill occasionally living there while they were away.

When Charlie returned to London in June 1912 following his first US tour with Karno – a total of twenty months away – he discovered that Sydney had married and let the Glenshaw Mansions flat go, a bitter disappointment for the younger brother, who during his absence had come to see the apartment as "a sort of shrine".

Chaplin would later remember: "This was a severe blow to me – to think that that cheerful little haven that had given substance to my sense of living, a pride in a home, was no more... I was homeless. I rented a back room in the Brixton Road. It was so dismal that I resolved to return to the United States as soon as possible."

After almost immediately touring France and the Channel Islands with the Karno troupe, Chaplin left for another American tour four months after discovering that Glenshaw Mansions had been let go; he would not return to England for nine years.

Charlie Chaplin's London

Sydney Chaplin

The blue plaque you see above the doorway was unveiled in June 2017 by the comedian Paul Merton.

....

Chaplin's Coffee shop next door, with its 1920s décor, has several prints of Charlie's film posters on its walls and is a good spot to stop for a refreshment.

If you have a few minutes to spare, continue walking along Brixton Road to your left until you reach the corner of Mowl Street, and feast your eyes on the magnificent Art Noveau-style Christ Church, built in 1902, with its wonderful outdoor pulpit on the far-left corner.

Retrace your steps back up Brixton Road and cross over South Island Place – note the ghostly 'Hovis' advert painted on the wall by some long-ago grocer, who may well have sold a loaf to Chaplin while he lived at Glenshaw Mansions – then turn left into Crewdson Road. Pass all the way along the street, lined almost completely by Victorian dwellings – compare these with the present-day tower blocks which hove into view as you near the end. At the end of Crewdson Street turn right into Clapham Road which, along with Brixton Road, is one of the major routes in and out of London from the south.

Walk on its right side for a few minutes, crossing

Handforth Road continuing past the wonderfully-named Pickle Mews (the Offley Works were the original home of J.A. Sharwood & Co.), until you reach the magnificent red-brick building of

13. THE BELGRAVE HOSPITAL FOR CHILDREN

First founded in Pimlico in 1866, the Belgrave Hospital for Children later relocated to this building which was constructed between 1899 and 1926.

The great music hall comedian Dan Leno, hugely admired by Chaplin, donated £625 to the hospital, of

which he was Vice President, during a visit on 20th October 1904 after what proved to be his final show, for he died eleven days later.

Belgrave Hospital for Children joined the NHS in 1948, and closed in 1985. Despite having been awarded Grade II listing status in 1981, the building was left unused until the 1990s, when it was converted into residential apartments.

Resume along Clapham Road. Cross Prima Road, and continue walking along with the railings on your right and the bus stop on your left. Pass St Mark's Church, which was built in 1824 on the site of the Surrey Gallows, where between 1678 and 1799 more than 140 people were executed.

[Note: If for some reason you need to end the tour at this point, cross over the road at the traffic lights to Oval Station (Northern line).]

To continue with the tour, go past St Mark's and just before the railings curve to the right cross over via the traffic lights, so that you are continuing to walk in the same direction, and just past the bus stop marked N pause at the memorial comprising a tall column with a golden ball on top.

This marks the spot where, for almost a century, the

Kennington Gate

Kennington Tollgate was situated, at which levies were collected from travellers into London from the roads south of the city. Look back towards St Mark's and compare the photograph of Kennington Gate overleaf with the scene as it is today, and note that the boarded-up kiosk you see before you is on the same spot as the historic stand.

Although the toll was abolished in 1865, the junction understandably was known locally for many years as

14. KENNINGTON GATE

It was here that, at the age of nineteen, Chaplin waiting nervously for the girl who had stolen his heart just days earlier: a young dancer named Hetty Kelly.

They had met while on the same bill at the Streatham Empire, where he was appearing with the Karno troupe and watched from the wings as the fifteen year old Hetty performed as part of Bert Coutts's Yankee Doodle Girls.

When one of her fellow dancers slipped and the others giggled, Hetty looked over at the young comic and their eyes met; when she afterwards came off stage and asked him to hold a mirror while she fixed her hair, Chaplin was smitten. As he was still in make-up for his act playing a middle-aged drunk, Hetty assumed he was much older than his years – 'at least thirty' – but nevertheless promised to meet him the following Sunday afternoon, here at Kennington Gate.

A few minutes before the agreed time of four o'clock, Chaplin waited here in nervous excitement. Suddenly, in a scene which could have come from one of his later comedies, he realised that he had never seen Hetty without stage make-up, so was uncertain what she actually looked like. For the next minute or two the nervous paramour anxiously scanned the face of every plain-looking girl who approached the spot,

Charlie Chaplin's London

Hetty Kelly

hoping not to be disappointed, until at last Hetty stepped from a tram, and Chaplin's heart was lost.

The following morning, and the next two after that, the couple met and held hands as they walked the short distance to the Underground station to make their way to their respective rehearsals. But things did not continue so idyllic for long: "Three mornings I had known her; three abbreviated little mornings which made the rest of the day non-existent, until the next morning. But on the fourth morning her manner changed. She met me coldly, without enthusiasm, and would not take my hand. I reproached her for it and jokingly accused her of not being in love with me."

And this was most probably the case; while Chaplin was filled with ideas of romance, love and marriage, Hetty was just fifteen and talk of such things alarmed her.

Their relationship lasted just eleven days, but it clearly meant a lot to Chaplin. He was able to recall, nearly fifty years later, that Hetty's face had smelled of Sunlight soap on one occasion when he had called at her house, and was distraught when, on his way to London for his 1921 homecoming visit, he learned from her brother that Hetty had died in the influenza epidemic of 1918.

Despite – or perhaps because of – this tragic news, as

part of his visit to his childhood haunts the following day Chaplin had a taxi take him to this spot, which held such bitter-sweet memories:

"I get out and stand there for a few moments on Kennington Gate. My taxi driver thinks I am mad. But I am forgetting taxi drivers. I am remembering a lad of nineteen, dressed to the pink, with fluttering heart, waiting, waiting for the moment of the day when he and happiness walked along the road. The road is so alluring now. It beckons for another walk, and as I hear a street car approaching I turn eagerly, for the moment almost expecting to see the same trim Hetty step off, smiling. The car stops. A couple of men get off. An old woman. Some children. But no Hetty. Hetty is gone. So is the lad with the frock coat and cane.'

Cross over to the perimeter of the park on your right via the double traffic lights, then turn left and follow the curve of the railings, with the park on your right. Continue along, walking with the long stretch of the brick-built apartments and the ground-floor shops running parallel on your left, until you come to the next major road junction, with traffic lights. Pause by the 'Kennington Park Road' sign affixed to the railings on your right and look over at the concrete and glass modern office block.

In the photograph opposite, the group of people on the pavement on the right are standing on the spot you are now. This corner was the site of

....

15. THE HORNS TAVERN AND ASSEMBLY ROOMS

A tavern was first recorded on this site in 1725, when it was known as the Green Man and Horns, a reference no doubt to what was at the time Kennington Common opposite. The Horns Tavern and the property alongside was purchased in 1811 by Richard Farmer, whose vitriol factory on the other side of the park was earning him great wealth. He sold the tavern on in 1822, after which the property was redeveloped a number of times, including the addition of an Assembly Hall to the left of the pub, which could accommodate 1,000 people.

Both the Horns and the Assembly Rooms were rebuilt in 1887, the version shown in the photograph, which is how they appeared when Chaplin booked the Assembly Rooms in 1907 to rehearse a comedy sketch he'd written titled 'Twelve Just Men'. It was, as Chaplin later described, "a slapstick affair about a jury arguing a case of breach of promise. One of the jurors was a

The Horns Tavern and Assembly Rooms c1905

deaf-mute, another a drunk and another a quack doctor."

After selling the script to a vaudeville hypnotist named Charcoate, a cast was engaged and they rehearsed for three days at the Assembly Rooms, until Chaplin received a note from Charcoate saying he'd decided not to produce it after all, and the sketch was off.

The seventeen year old Chaplin was too nervous to tell the cast, so they continued rehearsing until lunchtime, when he took them to his rooms, and hid in the kitchen while brother Sydney told the cast what had happened.

During his return to London in 1921 Chaplin revisited his old haunts, stopping for a drink in the Horns. He remembered it had been "rather elegant in its day, with its polished mahogany bar, fine mirrors and billiard room," but now found it a little seedy.

During WWII the Assembly Rooms were completely destroyed, with the Horns bar itself suffering damage but remaining open for a further twenty years. It was demolished in 1965.

Walk a few more steps so that the entrance to the park is on your right, then cross left over Kennington Park Road via the traffic lights towards the modern office block. On reaching the other side walk up Kennington Road, to the left of the modern office block, keeping to the right-hand side.

After the supermarket – which sits on the site of the Assembly Rooms – turn immediately right into Stannary Street, and pause to look over at the Grade II listed building now called The Lycée, a number of apartments converted in 2007, but formerly

16. KENNINGTON ROAD SCHOOL

An infrequent pupil, Chaplin had been enrolled for short spells in whatever school was nearest to where he was staying at any time, and this school was less than half a mile from the rooms where his father was living when Charlie and Sydney stayed with him while Hannah was in Cane Hill Asylum, during the late autumn of 1898.

Chaplin recalled that attending the Kennington Road School was a welcome diversion from the miserable existence at his father's home, where they were forced to live in cramped conditions with Charles Sr rarely at home, instead being trusted to the dubious care of the woman he lived with, known only to history as 'Louise'. "…the presence of other children made me feel less isolated. Saturday was a half-holiday, but I never looked forward to it because it meant going home and scrubbing floors and cleaning knives, and on that day Louise invariably started drinking."

But Chaplin began to take an interest in school after he had recited an amusing poem called 'Miss Priscilla's Cat' to a schoolfriend and it was observed by a teacher named Reid, who subsequently had the boy repeat it to every class at the school, resulting in a glow of celebrity.

Chaplin continued attending this establishment after

The Alderman
Courtesy National Brewery Heritage

leaving his father's care and moving to rooms with his mother – our next stop. His last appearance in the school's register was on 25th November 1898.

Many years later, on his return to London in 1921, after his drink at the Horns Chaplin walked to his former school and peered into the playground, noting – as all adults do – that it seemed to have shrunk.

Continue along Stannary Street, passing on your left the red-bricked former LCC Gas Meter Testing Station and what was a public house (the Craven Arms 1852-73, renamed the Alderman 1873-2003). Go all the way to the end, and cross over Ravenston Street into Radcot Street, which becomes Methley Street as it bends round to the left.

This area, built in 1868, has the feel of a lovely warm Victorian community – if only it wasn't for the cars!

Continue to the end, on the left-hand side, crossing over Milverton Street, and stop at the second-to-last house on the left just as the road bends to the right, which bears a blue plaque. This is

17. 39 METHLEY STREET

When Hannah had been discharged from Cane Hill Asylum and collected her boys from their father's house in November 1898, it was here at 39 Methley Street that they made a home, renting one simple but cheap room for nine months. They seemed to enjoy a relatively comfortable existence, with Charles Sr

for now making regular maintenance payments and Hannah resuming her needlework.

Chaplin later recalled the acrid smell from the nearby Hayward's pickle factory, wafting over Kennington Cross from their premises on Montford Place.

One particular incident from this time appears to have stayed with him for a long time. The building behind you to the right, which is now the Camera Club premises, was formerly a slaughterhouse. Sheep would frequently be driven there along Methley Street, and one afternoon, as Chaplin watched them pass, one escaped from the flock and ran off. The shambolic attempts of the slaughtermen to catch the animal made him laugh, but as it was finally caught and carried off to the abattoir the reality of what was about to happen filled Chaplin with horror, and he ran inside screaming for his mother.

He would later write: "I wonder if that episode did not establish the premise of my future films – the combination of the tragic and the comic." It has been suggested that Methley Street was the visual inspiration for Chaplin's *Easy Street*.

With your back to Chaplin's house, walk along what is now Bowden Street, passing the Camera Club on your left. At its end pause to look across at the magisterial Lambeth County Court. Turn left into Cleaver Street, walking along its left-hand side, and stop at the end of the road.
On the opposite corner is the Tommyfield Pub, in Chaplin's day called

18. THE WHITE HART

It was during the six-week period that he lived with his father, between September and November 1898, that a nine year old Chaplin spent one particularly miserable Saturday evening wandering around this area – called Kennington Cross – after finding himself alone, the nearby lodgings where the family were staying empty, dark and forbidding.

As the night wore on, Chaplin sat on the kerb on the other side of the road to where you are now, in front of the building with the cream triangular portico supported by four columns, watching the house for signs of activity, feeling hungry, tired and utterly wretched. All the lights of the shops began to be extinguished, and the streets became deserted.

Then, as Chaplin later recalled, "Suddenly there was music. Raptuous! It came from the vestibule of the White Hart corner pub, and resounded brilliantly across the empty square. The tune was 'The Honeysuckle and the Bee', played with radiant virtuosity on a harmonium and clarinet. I had never been conscious of melody before, but this one was beautiful and lyrical, so blithe and gay, so warm and reassuring. I forgot my despair and crossed the road to where the musicians were. The harmonium player was blind, with scarred sockets where the eyes had been;

and a besotted, embittered face played the clarinet. It was all over too soon and their exit left the night even sadder."

First opened in 1746 and rebuilt in 1897 to this design, the White Hart was closed in 2010 for major refurbishment, reopening as the Tommyfield.

....

Walk around the pub, passing its front door, so that you are walking up Kennington Lane with the shops on your right.

The first shop to the left of the Tommyfield – after the door to the flats – is now a large estate agent's which takes up three shop widths, but in 1898 was a cook-shop to which Chaplin was sent to buy a shilling's worth of corned beef by his father's common-law wife Louise on the first day he and Sydney arrived to live with them. The flats above reveal the narrowness of the old shops.

From this vantage point is it possible to see the original name of the White Hart high up in the ornate fascia. Continue along, past the postbox, and stop at the glorious

....

19. DURNING LIBRARY

Designed to a Gothic Revival style by Sidney Smith, the architect of the Tate Britain art gallery eight years later, the Durning Library opened in 1889. It was gifted to the people of Southwark by the

Charlie Chaplin's London

philanthropist Jemina Durning Smith, daughter of the Anti-Corn Law League founding chairman John Benjamin Smith.

Grade II listed in 1981, the building benefits from the promotional activities of the Friends of Durning Library (www.durninglibraryfriends.org.uk).

....

 Retrace your steps to the Tommyfield, and cross at the traffic lights right over Kennington Lane.

On the traffic island note the Victorian gentlemen's lavatory, opened in 1898 and in use until 1988. Since 2001 the structure has been Grade II listed, and following a period of fundraising running water and electricity were installed in 2013. For the next four years it operated as a community arts centre, ArtsLav.

Near the railings is a tall, narrow black column topped by a golden crown. Can you guess what it is? Well, suffice to say, in Victorian times the aroma emanating from the capital's underground lavatories was a bit of a problem. Resourceful as ever, our engineering predecessors built these columns, called stinkpipes, to take the revolting smell up and over the heads of the ladies and gentlemen walking by. These pipes can be seen dotted around London's streets, but none are perhaps as lovely as this fine example.

Cross the narrow cobbled road to stand outside

20. THE DOG HOUSE

Known as the Roebuck since at least the 1850s, it was under that name that Chaplin would have remembered this pub when he regularly passed by its doors while living with his father three doors along in the autumn of 1898.

The comic would later recall with sadness how he felt despondent lying on his bed at night while the sounds of a concertina passed the bedroom window, accompanied by rowdy young men and giggling girls, his misery deepening as the happy sounds grew fainter as the group disappeared up the street. Chaplin recalled on one occasion hearing the customers leaving the Roebuck at closing time, happy drunks singing a popular song of the time titled 'For Old Times' Sake', which included the agreeable lines "Life's too short to quarrel, Hearts are too precious to break. Shake hands and let us be friends, For old times' sake."

In more recent years the pub was renamed first the Charlie Chaplin, and now the Dog House – a large pub with plenty of character which is well worth a visit if time allows.

> *Walk left around the pub's hedged seating area, into Kennington Road, and stop at the first gate you come to – the house with the red door. This is*

21. 287 KENNINGTON ROAD

With the briefness of Hannah and Charles Chaplin's marriage, the couple being together for just over two years following their son's birth, by the time he was nine the young Chaplin could only remember having seen his father once, when he happened to be passing this house when a man and a woman walked down the path.

Sensing this man was his father, Chaplin stopped on the spot which you are now standing as they approached. The man obviously recognised the boy, for he asked his name and, receiving the answer 'Charlie Chaplin', gave a knowing look to the woman by his side. He reached into his pocket and gave his son half a crown, which the younger Chaplin grasped and ran home to tell his mother that he had just met his father.

The second occasion had much more serious ramifications, for it was here to 287 Kennington Road, into the care of their father, that Charlie and Sydney were sent from the Lambeth Workhouse when

Charlie Chaplin's London

their mother was transferred to Cane Hill Asylum in September 1898.

They were transported from the workhouse in a bread van, and as their father was not at home the paperwork was signed by the woman that Charlie had seen with his father that day walking down the path – his common-law wife, whom he later described as "dissipated and morose-looking, yet attractive, tall and shapely, with full lips and sad, doe-like eyes; her age could have been thirty. Her name was Louise."

Going upstairs to the first floor where they had two rooms, in the front sitting-room – the windows you can see from your vantage point – Chaplin saw a young boy of around four with brown eyes and brown curly hair; Louise's son, and his half-brother.

Chaplin later described the accommodation as 'sad', with the large front windows admitting dim light which appeared filtered as if underwater, with tired horse-hair furniture, tired wallpaper, and a glass case on the wall which contained a stuffed pike which had a second pike, as large as itself, emerging from its mouth. According to Chaplin, both pike looked 'gruesomely sad'.

The uneasy relationship between Charlie, Sydney and Louise got off to a bad start when Sydney complained that the single bed in the back room meant for he and Charlie to share was too small, to which Louise responded that they would sleep where they were told to. Within minutes she sent the boys to do errands, Charlie being dispatched to the cook-shop next to the White Hart for corned beef.

When Charles Sr came home he was pleased to see his sons, and Charlie in particular watched his father's every move with fascination. But in the few weeks they stayed in his care Chaplin Sr was rarely home, and when he was he was often drunk. Louise, too, would escape the fraught situation thrust upon her each weekend by drinking to excess.

On the Saturday evening that Chaplin heard 'The Honeysuckle and the Bee' emanating from the White Hart, he had arrived back from the half-day at school only to find himself locked out. He subsequently spent several hours wandering around aimlessly, drifting along Lambeth Walk and as far as Waterloo, before returning home and sitting on the kerbside to wait.

At last he saw a figure shuffling along the path towards the front door; it was Louise, completely drunk. As Chaplin started up the stairs hoping to slip into bed unnoticed, she suddenly turned on him and shouted that he was not welcome in the house. At this, the youngster ran down to the path and off to find his father. Within a few minutes he saw him staggering towards him, and back in the rooms an almighty row broke out, culminating in Charles Sr throwing a heavy clothes-brush at her, striking her on the side of the face.

Although Charlie and Sydney stayed with their father for just six weeks, it was a miserable existence for all concerned and it was a relief when Hannah was discharged from Cane Hill on 12th November and collected her sons, setting up home in the comparative sanctuary of Methley Street. Chaplin never saw his half-brother again.

Kennington Road has a happier connection, one which his father was instrumental in arranging.

A few doors along, at No. 267, lived an acquaintance of Charles Sr named William Jackson, who was the founder of a popular clog-dancing troupe called the Eight Lancashire Lads, who regularly toured the country. He was persuaded to take on Charlie, and when Hannah was told that her son would receive board and lodging while on tour, and she half a crown a week, she readily agreed. It the start of Charlie Chaplin's career as a paid entertainer, and although, like the rest of the Lads, he had his mind set on a solo career, the youngster recognised it was a good opportunity to gain experience – and money.

Years later, Jackson's youngest son Alfred, a year

Charlie Chaplin during his time with the Eight Lancashire Lads

older than Chaplin, remembered the new boy: "He was a very quiet boy at first, and, considering that he didn't come from Lancashire, wasn't a bad dancer. My first job was to take him to have his hair, which was hanging in matted curls about his shoulders, cut to a reasonable length."

Continue walking along Kennington Road for a few steps then cross over to the other side via the pelican crossing. On the other side turn left and then right at Tesco into Black Prince Road.

On the night that Louise had thrown Chaplin out in a drunken rage, the young Charlie walked down this street towards the Queen's Head pub, where he expected to find his father, and we follow in his footsteps now.

Cross to the left side when safe to do so, and continue for several minutes along this road, which is a curiosity in that nearly all the buildings along its left-hand side are Victorian, while those on the right are modern. So, as my old Sergeant Major used to say, "Eyes Left!"

On the corner of Newburn Street, filling the next block, is the Grade II listed almshouses complex Woodstock Court, built in 1914 as the Old Tenant's Hostel built for elderly tenants of the Duchy of Cornwall estate.

Bas relief on the Beaufoy Institute

A little further along is the splendid red-brick Beaufoy Institute, opened in 1907. Henry Beaufoy, whose family had made its money initially in gin but changed the use *of their Lambeth factory to the production of vinegar, built the Lambeth Ragged School on Newport Road, off the Black Prince Road, in 1850/51 as a memorial to his wife. Alongside Henry Beaufoy on the Board of Trustees was John Doulton, of the world-famous ceramics company also based in Lambeth, and we are heading towards their premises now. The Beaufoy site was sold to the London and Metropolitan Railway Company and the trustees eventually settled on this new location for the Institute, which served as a technical institute for boys. The foundation stone was laid by Mildred Beaufoy, wife of George's nephew Mark Hanbury Beaufoy, who was by now chairman of the governors. During WWII the building was used to manufacture munitions, many local women being employed here, after the conflict passing to Lambeth Council. The building was sold to the Diamond Way Buddhism group in 2014, and continues to exude a certain tranquillity today.*

Continue along Black Prince Road, passing the park on your left, and at the next junction is

22. THE JOLLY GARDENERS

With its appearance as a typical back-street London pub, the Jolly Gardeners has provided a location for the films *Snatch* and *The Calcium Kid*, but also has links to the London-born early movie star who is the subject of our walk.

Local tradition holds that down Lilac Place, the little alley to the right of the pub, is the cellar door on which the young Chaplin practised tap dancing. Now metal, but once made of wood, it is easy to imagine the youngster entertaining a crowd of admiring onlookers on this spot.

Pints have been served here since around 1750, although the building was rebuilt in 1895 to what we see today, and would be certainly recognisable

Lilac Place, with the Jolly Gardners on the right

to Charlie Chaplin. The pub was renamed the Jolly Cockney for a period in the 1980s, reverting to its original moniker a decade or so later. Now a German-themed bar serving Bavarian bangers and beer, a rather old upright piano at the rear of the pub is said to have been played by both Chaplin and his father, depending on who tells the story.

Continue along Black Prince Road for a couple of minutes, past the row of shops, until the next junction and

23. THE QUEEN'S HEAD

Serving thirsty customers from at least 1780, the Queen's Head was rebuilt to its current design in 1890. From the following year it was run by Chaplin's uncle Spencer until his death in 1900.

Spencer Chaplin seems to have been a successful businessman; he ran a number of local taverns, and in November 1897 paid the considerable sum of £44 7s to the Southwark Board of Guardians on behalf of his younger brother Charles, the comedian's father, representing unpaid maintenance payments for the upkeep of his sons, thereby averting his arrest.

The Queen's Head has a more tangible link with the Chaplin story. It was here that a local character named Archibald Binks – known to one and all as 'Rummy' – would wait outside, and would fetch the horses from the nearby cab rank for their drivers as they emerged from within, for which he would be tipped a penny.

Years later Chaplin recalled: "He had a bulbous nose, a crippled-up rheumatic body, a swollen and distorted pair of feet and the most extraordinary pair of trousers I ever saw. He must have got the trousers from a giant, and he was a little man. When I saw Rummy shuffle his way across the pavement to hold a cabman's horse for a penny tip, I was fascinated. The walk was so funny to me that I imitated it. When I showed my mother how Rummy walked, she begged me to stop because it was cruel to imitate a misfortune like that. But she pleaded while she had her apron stuffed into her mouth. Then she went into the pantry and giggled for ten minutes. Day after day I cultivated that walk. It became an obsession. Whenever I pulled it, I was sure of a laugh. Now no matter what else I may do that is amusing, I can never get away from the walk."

The Queen's Head turned off its taps in 2011, and is now a café. There is a large print of Chaplin adorning an inside wall, and his image graces the menu.

This stop marks two-thirds of our tour, so if you are

in need of a rest this is a good place to do so. Tucked behind the Queen's Head – accessed via Vauxhall Road to its left – is the entrance to the peaceful Pedlar's Park, a lovely spot to sit with a coffee and a sandwich if the weather is good.

Before you take your leave of the Queen's Head, look over the railway bridge on your left to view the looming Doulton factory, which was built between 1876-78. In fact, this building is the single survivor of what was originally a vast complex comprising four factory buildings – this surviving corner was the company's showroom.

If you have time to spare, it really is worth the walk under the railway bridge to examine the building in its full majesty. If you do, make sure to examine the wonderful ceramic plaques which dot the walls on both sides under the bridge, and to look up at the bas relief of factory workers above the central doorway. The building is now warehouse offices.

Retrace your steps past the Queen's Head, returning to the Jolly Gardeners, and with your back to the pub cross the road via the zebra crossing. Enter the pedestrianised path into the world-famous Lambeth Walk.

This street, once a bustling hive of activity, was arguably

Charlie Chaplin's London

Bas relief above the entrance to the Doulton Factory

the most famous in London, thanks to the song of the same name, and as we have heard the young Chaplin wandered aimlessly along this thoroughfare on the day he found himself locked out of his father's lodgings.

There was already a market in Lambeth Walk by the 1860s, similar to that seen earlier in the tour at East Street, selling everything from fish, meat and vegetables to clothing and ornaments along more than 200 yards of stalls.

Locals who took to promenading along the length of the market inspired the songwriter E.W. Rogers to pen 'The Lambeth Walk' in 1899, which was performed by Arthur Hurley, Marie Lloyd's second husband. The performers met while on the same tour of Australia in 1901, Hurley singing 'The Lambeth Walk'.

The different song of the same name which is much better known today was written for the 1937 musical Me And My Girl, the music composed by Noel Gay and lyrics by Douglas Furber and L. Arthur Rose. The musical proved immediately popular, and continues to be performed today. Lambeth Walk was severely damaged during the War (footage can be found on the British Pathe website at britishpathe.com, and was rebuilt in the current nondescript style.

As there's little of note along the five minute stroll along Lambeth Walk – bar five interesting mounted murals

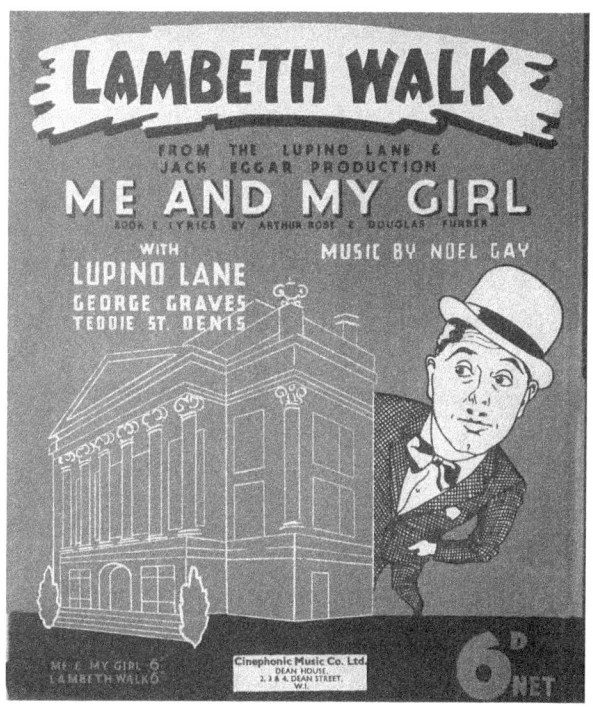

dating from the 1980s halfway along on your right-hand side – I suggest you entertain yourself by singing the song as you partake in a little bit of promenading yourself. Take care to keep an eye open for Fitzalan Street, on the right-hand side, which is almost where you will take your next turn!

Edgar's Guide To...

Anytime you're Lambeth way
Any evening, any day,
You'll find us all doin' the Lambeth walk.
Ev'ry little Lambeth gal
With her little Lambeth pal,
You'll find 'em all doin' the Lambeth walk.

Ev'rything's free and easy,
Do as you darn well pleasey,
Why don't you make your way there,
Go there, stay there,
Once you get down Lambeth way,
Ev'ry evening, ev'ry day,
You'll find yourself doin' the Lambeth walk.

Anytime you're Lambeth way
Any evening, any day,
You'll find us all doin' the Lambeth walk.
Ev'ry little Lambeth gal
With her little Lambeth pal,
You'll find 'em all doin' the Lambeth walk.

Ev'rything's free and easy,
Do as you darn well pleasey,
Why don't you make your way there,
Go there, stay there.

Charlie Chaplin's London

Once you get down Lambeth way,
Ev'ry evening, ev'ry day,
You'll find yourself doin' the Lambeth walk.

Anytime you're Lambeth way
Any evening, any day,
You'll find us all doin' the Lambeth walk.

Ev'ry little Lambeth gal
With her little Lambeth pal,
You'll find 'em all doin' the Lambeth walk.

Ev'rything's free and easy,
Do as you darn well pleasey,
Why don't you make your way there,
Go there, stay there.

Once you get down Lambeth way,
Ev'ry evening, ev'ry day,
You'll find yourself
Doin' the Lambeth –
Doin' the Lambeth –
Doin' the Lambeth walk!

Continue along Lambeth Walk almost to the end: once you pass the turn into Fitzalan Street on your right you will start to see the surviving Victorian buildings.

At the next right, turn into the narrow and wonderfully-named Walnut Tree Walk, with what was the Lambeth Tavern on the left corner – no doubt a lively evening out in its heyday.

As you pass down Walnut Tree Walk note the LCC housing Derby and Minton Houses on your left, with the primary school built in 1873 on your right, alongside which is St Olave's House (1884). Immediately after St Olave's House are Nos. 9,10&11 Walnut Tree Walk, built in the middle of the eighteenth century and refronted in the early part of the nineteenth. All three residences are Grade II listed. After the post-war redevelopment of Lambeth Walk, we are now back among characterful historical buildings.

Near the end, on the left side, is a red-brick building dated 1901 which marks the corner of a complex of apartments which would have been very familiar to Chaplin.

Turn left at the corner into Kennington Road, walk a few steps and then pause at the entrance on your left to the majestic Walcott Gardens, formerly known as

24. WALCOTT MANSIONS

During Hannah Chaplin's days on the south London stages she had become friendly with Jessie McNally, an Irish singer and dancer. The same year Charlie Jr was born – 1889 – Jessie married Walter McCarthy, an accountant, and the couple soon welcomed a son, Walter Jr, and a daughter, Norah.

Although the friends lost touch for a number of years, when the McCarthys moved to an apartment here at Walcott Mansions (which, as we have seen with the building around the corner dated 1901, were newly-built), Charlie and Walter Jr – known as 'Wally' – became great friends, and the young Chaplin subsequently spent a lot of time here.

He later recalled how the two boys would play 'theatre' at the back of the building, Chaplin always casting himself as the villain as he knew "instinctively they were more colourful than the hero." More often than not he was invited to stay for supper, leaving Hannah alone in the miserable room which the Chaplins were renting nearby.

When Mrs McCarthy became ill and died early in 1903, aged just 35, the naïve Chaplin made an attempt to persuade his mother, who was at this time beginning to again show signs of mental illness, to smarten herself up so that Mr McCarthy would want to marry her, hoping that not only would Hannah be happy, but that he and Wally could see more of each other. He told her, to his later deep regret, "If you were all dressed up and made yourself attractive, as you used to be, he would. But you don't make any effort; all you do is sit around this filthy room and look awful."

One afternoon soon afterwards, on 5th May 1903, Chaplin was again invited to lunch at Walcott Mansions, but decided instead to return home to see his mother.

When he arrived, neighbours told him that Hannah had "gone mad"; when the local doctor arrived he agreed, and sent her to Lambeth Infirmary, from where she was transferred again to Cane Hill Asylum – this time staying for seven months.

Walter McCarthy did marry again – not to Hannah, but to Ethel Bryant, in 1905. Chaplin's friend Wally tragically died aged just nineteen, in 1909.

....

Once you have feasted your eyes on Walcott Gardens, continue along Kennington Road for a few minutes then cross over at the traffic lights on your right towards the pub on the other side of the road. Once there, pause outside

....

Charlie Chaplin's London

Walter McCarthy Sr
©*Sheila Evans*

25. THE TANKARD

It was the habit of vaudeville performers in the late Victorian era to take a pony and trap out for a drive on a Sunday morning along the Kennington Road, stopping at hostelries such as the Horns Tavern and this, the Tankard. As a boy of twelve Chaplin would often stand on this pavement, watching them step down from their rig and enter the lounge bar, where the elite of vaudeville met.

He would later recall, "How glamorous they were, dressed in chequered suits and grey bowlers, flashing their diamond rings and tie pins! At two o'clock on

The Tankard, 1880s

Sunday afternoon, the pub closed and its occupants filed outside and dallied awhile before bidding each other adieu; and I would gaze fascinated and amused, for some of them swaggered with a ridiculous air. When the last had gone his way, it was as though the sun had gone through a cloud. And I would return to a row of old derelict houses that sat back off the Kennington Road, to 3 Pownall Terrace, and mount the rickety stairs that led to our small garret."

The Tankard appears to have opened in the 1820s, and has continued to refresh visitors of all callings since, not just those treading the boards. Following name changes to the Grand Union and Bar Room Bar, the Tankard reopened under its original name in 2017.

....

Follow the curve of the Tankard to the left of its front door, into Brook Drive, and continue along this fine example of a Victorian terrace for a few minutes, with the symbol of the 21st century looming on the horizon.

Take the first left into Austral Street, with the former Two Eagles public house on its right-hand corner. This road appears to present a more prosperous neighbourhood, and is indeed representative of a happier time in the

Chaplins' lives.

Proceed to the end of Austral Street, passing on your left the All Saints Annex – once an orphan's home – and enter genteel West Square, making your way on your left around the gardens, noting the blue plaque to scientist J.A.R. Newlands, the chemist who discovered the Periodic Law of elements, who was born and raised at No. 19.

Continue around the gardens and pause outside No. 39, with the white door.

---

26. WEST SQUARE

It was of these comfortable surroundings that Chaplin had his earliest memory. Soon after his son was born, Charles Sr saw his career begin to blossom; he was regularly booked for engagements, and had five of his songs published within eighteen months. At what must have been a very happy time in the Chaplins' lives, they moved to rooms here at 39 West Square.

But this growing success in Chaplin Sr's career would be at a price. In the summer of 1890, when his son was just a year old, the entertainer was invited to undertake a three-month tour of America, starting in New York in August.

When he returned, the relationship between Mr and Mrs Chaplin appears to have broken down. Hannah soon formed a friendship with George Dryden Wheeler, an entertainer who performed under the name Leo Dryden. A son, George Dryden Wheeler Jr, was born on 31st August 1892 – another half-brother to Charlie Chaplin.

Although the future movie star would later write that the family were able to continue living here at West Square due to their mother being booked for a number of engagements, there are no records of Hannah appearing on any stage during this period.

The likelihood is that she and the boys were being supported by Leo Dryden, but this arrangement stopped abruptly in the summer of 1893, when Dryden took his six month old son and abandoned his lover. At this time Charlie was four and Sydney seven; neither would see their half-brother for thirty years, until he wrote to them after Chaplin had become world famous in America, and Leo Dryden told his son the truth. The third brother joined Charlie and Sydney in America, and forged his own career under the name 'Wheeler Dryden'.

Back in 1893, with the cessation of financial support Hannah had no choice but to leave West Square and move to much humbler accommodation.

Wheeler Dryden, half-brother of Charlie Chaplin

Years later, Chaplin would return to this serene enclosure, with its beautiful gardens and happy memories, and remark: "As I walk around West Square, I come upon a stationer's shop where they sell toys, sweets and tobacco. The store has an odour that awakens memories. It smells Christmassy. In the window I see a Noah's ark with painted wooden animals. I can't resist it. I go in and buy it just to get a whiff of the paint and the feel of the excelsior that's packed inside."

☞ *Complete your circuit of West Square, exiting again into Austral Square. At the end turn left to resume your walk along Brook Drive. Pause by the second lamppost and look over the road at the red-brick building with the blue gates; now flats, but in Chaplin's time the site of*

27. LAMBETH INFIRMARY

Opened in 1876, the Lambeth Infirmary was built on a site adjacent to the Lambeth Workhouse, which had been opened five years earlier. It was here that the sick of the borough were sent by their doctor to receive treatment.

Hannah Chaplin was received here at the Infirmary

Rear view of Lambeth Hospital, 1937
© *London Metropolitan Archives*

for the first time on 6th September 1898 with mental ill-health, being transferred to Cane Hill Asylum nine days later for treatment. Charlie brought his mother here for the same reason in May 1903, having returned home from school to be told that Hannah had gone insane. A doctor was called, and he scribbled a note to that effect which Charlie was to hand to the medics at the Infirmary. Chaplin later recalled:

"As we left the house, the neighbours and children were gathered at the front gate, looking on with awe. The infirmary was about a mile away. As we ambled along Mother staggered like a drunken woman from weakness, veering from side to side as I supported her. The stark afternoon sun seemed to ruthlessly expose our misery. People who passed us must have thought Mother was drunk, but to me they were like phantoms in a dream. She never spoke, but seemed to know where we were going and to be anxious to get there. On the way I tried to reassure her, and she smiled, too weak to talk. When at last we arrived at the infirmary a young doctor took her in charge. After reading the note, he said kindly, 'All right Mrs Chaplin, come this way.'"

Charlie's grandfather Charles Hill had also spent a memorable fortnight here, in July 1899, as a result of his crippling rheumatism. He had been living with his daughter and grandsons in their Methley Street room, unable to continue his work as a shoemaker. While in the infirmary, according to Chaplin he amused the nurses by telling them – no doubt with a wink – that, despite the rheumatism, "not all his machinery was impaired". When able to, Grandfather Hill was put to work in the infirmary kitchen, and as a result whenever Hannah or Charlie visited they were surreptitiously passed a bag of eggs, which they smuggled out hidden within their clothing. Said Chaplin later, "It was a sorry day for us when Grandpa was rid of his rheumatism and left the hospital."

Another inmate of both Lambeth Infirmary and

the workhouse was Mary Ann Nichols, generally believed to have been the first victim of the infamous 'Jack the Ripper'. She was regularly admitted here throughout the 1800s, and indeed when her body was found she was wearing two petticoats with 'Lambeth Workhouse' stencilled upon them.

In the early Twentieth century affordable social housing became more readily available, as we have seen during our tour, and as a result there was more space at the Lambeth Workhouse than was required, but not enough at the Infirmary. Consequently, in 1922 the two institutions were amalgamated to become Lambeth Hospital, under the control of the medical superintendent and matron of the infirmary. Over the following decade facilities were dramatically improved, and by 1939 Lambeth Hospital could accommodate 1,250 patients, and was among the largest hospitals in London. It eventually closed in 1976, and the majority of the site demolished and replaced with housing. Thankfully, the central block of the Lambeth Workhouse still survives – for now.

Resume walking along Brook Drive. Cross over Hayles Street, then cross over towards the post box. On the other side, continue along Brook Drive then follow the pavement as it curves into Dante Road, staying on the right-hand side.

After a minute or two take the first right into George Mathers Road, walking towards the modern development, then at the end turn left and walk up the steps in the corner and follow the pedestrian path straight ahead until you come to the Cinema Museum on your right, known to Charlie Chaplin all too well as

....

28. LAMBETH WORKHOUSE

This area is now the other side of the Lambeth Hospital site, and was originally the workhouse which opened in 1871, accommodating 820 inmates on a site of over seven acres. Very little of the building survives; the block before you, now the entrance to the Cinema Museum, was the administrative block. To the left of this was the male wing, with the female wing to the right. The tall erection peeping over the modern rooftops was formerly the shared water tower for the workhouse and infirmary, and is now converted into residential apartments.

It was into this segregated system that Hannah, Sydney and Charlie were admitted on 22nd July 1898, trudging the three-quarters of a mile from their humble lodgings on Farmer's Road. Chaplin later remembered their arrival:

"Although we were aware of the shame of going to the workhouse, when Mother told us about it both Sydney and I thought it adventurous and a change from living in one stuffy room.

But on that doleful day I didn't realise what was happening until we actually entered the workhouse gate [behind you, with the two brick columns]. Then the forlorn bewilderment of it struck me; for there we were made to separate,. Mother going in one direction to the women's ward and we in another to the children's."

A few days later they were permitted to meet in the shared Visiting Room, with Charlie and Sydney shocked at Hannah appearing in workhouse clothing. As for the boys, they also had succumbed to the workhouse 'uniform', having had their hair cropped.

They began to weep, which set their mother off too. Eventually they sat together on a bench, Hannah stroking her sons' shorn heads, all the while consoling them that they would be together again soon. She had earned a small amount of money by crocheting lace cuffs for one of the nurses, and had been able to buy some coconut candy from the workhouse store. When they were parted all too soon, Sydney repeatedly commented on how she had aged.

After eight days the boys were transferred to

*Entrance to Lambeth Workhouse, right,
with the boiler room and water tower centre, 1933*
© *London Metropolitan Archives*

Norwood Schools in Hanwell while Hannah remained here at Renfrew Road, but on 12th August enjoying their day together at Kennington Park before being re-admitted.

The suriving administration block of Lambeth Workhouse has, since 1998, been home to the wonderful Cinema Museum, which displays film memorabilia, movie posters and historic cinema uniforms, and of course Charlie Chaplin-related material. It is open for tours by appointment only, so if you would like to visit the Museum please call 020 7840 2200 or email info@cinemamuseum.org.uk to book a spot.

After exploring the Cinema Museum follow the front entrance out onto Dugard Way, between the two imposing brick columns with black gates which formed the workhouse entrance, and note the former Court Tavern (1874-2000), a lovely old Victorian building, on the right-hand corner. Turn left onto Renfrew Road and immediately admire the building that was

29. KENNINGTON COURTHOUSE

Built in 1869 as the Lambeth Police Court to a design

Charlie Chaplin's London

Lambeth Magistrates' Court, with the Court Tavern, in 1973

by the architect Thomas Sorby, the site includes a two-storey cell block, and is the oldest surviving criminal courthouse in London. It later became Lambeth Magistrates' Court, no doubt many defendants enjoying a drink in the Court Tavern on the opposite corner. The last case was heard here in the 1970s, before Camberwell Green Magistrates' Court was opened and business transferred there.

The building was purchased by the Jamyang Buddhist Centre in 1995, and the Dalai Lama visited four years later. The Centre's courtyard garden was previously the prisoners' exercise yard, and retains its Victorian cobblestones.

Next to this is

30. THE OLD KENNINGTON FIRE STATION

Built for the Metropolitan Fire Brigade by the Metropolitan Board of Works in 1868, the station opened for business two years later. When the Brigade adopted motorised fire engines after WWII, fewer stations were required and fifteen were closed in 1920, including Kennington. The Grade II listed building is now a number of very expensive apartments.

Kennington Fire Station 1904
© *London Metropolitan Archives*

For a better view – including of the tower in the building's centre – cross to the opposite side of Renfrew Road.

Retrace your steps to the Cinema Museum, and walk along the pedestrian footpath to the right of the building, then take the steps at the end and turn right back into George Mathers Road. Turn left at the end onto Dante

Road, walk to the end and turn right into Brook Drive.

Immediately cross over and turn left into Elliott's Row, another wonderful Victorian street, dominated on the right-hand side by the spectacular Hayles Buildings, tenements built between 1891 and 1902. At the end turn left into St George's Road, and admire the six-storey Saint George Buildings, another tenement block built in 1900.

Continue along this road for several minutes, crossing Hayles Street and the entrance to West Square, and passing Charlotte Sharman Primary Foundation School, built in 1884/85 and named after its founder, a Christian philanthropist.

Cross the narrow Geraldine Street, then continue along with the dark brick wall of the Imperial War Museum grounds on your left.

As you reach the bus stop labelled M look over the road to admire Notre Dame School, an all girls' Roman Catholic school built at the very end of the nineteenth century.

Continue to the next junction, with St George's Cathedral on the opposite corner, and turn left into Lambeth Road, keeping the railings on your left. You will soon pass the main entrance to the Imperial War Museum, and you should here return if you wish to visit the Museum after the end of our tour.

Just after you pass the Cygnet Churchill Hospital, an in-patient mental health facility for men on the other side of the road, cross to the right-hand side at the zebra crossing. On the other side turn left and immediately go over King Edward Walk.

A few houses along, No. 100 bears a blue plaque to William Bligh, the captain of the Bounty cast adrift in the infamous mutiny led by Fletcher Christian. Bligh lived in the house from its construction in 1794 (as 3 Durham Place) until 1813 following his wife's death.

Continue walking down Lambeth Road, and on the corner is our final stop on our tour of Charlie Chaplin's London,

31. THE THREE STAGS

Before entering this pub, which first appears in records in 1825, look up at the hanging sign, behind which you'll see street art depicting Chaplin with a pot of paint, seemingly having just daubed a blue CND symbol on the wall.

The Three Stags is a poignant spot to end our tour, as it was the scene for Chaplin's last meeting with his father, in early April 1901.

The Three Stags c1910

Although it was not a pub that Chaplin Sr frequented often, if at all, as his son was walking past one evening for some reason he had an urge to poke his head in the door to see if his father was there. Sure enough he was sitting in the corner, and when he saw his son beckoned him over.

Years of heavy drinking had caught up with Charles Chaplin Sr, and his body had swollen terribly with dropsy, no doubt caused by liver failure, and his breathing was laboured. Nevertheless, he seemed delighted to see his son, and spent some time enquiring about Hannah and Sydney.

Before the younger Chaplin left, his father took him in his arms and kissed him – the first and only time he did so.

Three weeks after this chance meeting Charles Chaplin Sr was taken to St Thomas's Hospital, half a mile from here. According to his son, he fought against being admitted when he realised where he was being taken.

He died ten days later, on 9th May 1901, aged just 37, and was buried in a pauper's grave at Tooting Cemetery, the funeral expenses met by his younger brother Albert, who had made a success of horse ranches in South Africa and happened to be in London.

The corner table at which it is believed the touching encounter between father and son took place is today called Chaplin's Corner, enclosed in its own mahogany and frosted-glass partitioned nook, and you can sit there awhile as you enjoy your own drink and contemplate the haunts of Charlie Chaplin's boyhood you have just visited. However, the Corner is very popular, so it is advisable to reserve the table in advance of your visit, if possible. Call 020 7928 5974 or visit www.thethreestags.com.

☙ ❧

It is here that I must leave you, my footsore cinematic history-seekers. I hope you have enjoyed this trip to the haunts of Charlie Chaplin's youth, and remember – no matter how tough your present situation may be, how humble your beginnings, great opportunity always lies ahead. Just keep swinging that cane and shuffling those shoes!

Pip, pip!
Edgar

On leaving the Three Stags, should you wish to visit the Imperial War Museum simply cross over the road via the traffic lights and turn left – the entrance to the grounds is on your right after a few minutes' walk. Then, on leaving the Museum, exit via the same gates and turn right, follow the road to the next junction and turn right into St George's Road, keeping the park on your right. Following this road will take you all the way back to the Elephant and Castle roundabout and tube station.

Alternatively, if you wish to make your way to the nearest Underground station after leaving the Three Stags, on leaving the pub turn right and walk along Kennington Road. After a couple of minutes you will pass Kennington Police Station; keep walking, and at the end of the road pause to look at the Oasis Centre on your right, which incorporates Christ Church.

The present version was built in the late 1950s following war damage to the original church, and only the Lincoln Tower from 1876, which rises above the Centre, remains. Its spire is unusual, in that its design features a stars and stripes pattern in honour of the assassinated President. It was here that Chaplin's mother worshipped each Sunday, with Charlie complaining how he had to join her in listening to Bach and the Rev. F.B. Meyer's fervent address to his flock. He later recalled how, at one hot summer's Holy Communion, he had enjoyed the 'grape juice' being passed along a little too much – and Hannah's restraining hand calling 'time'.

Cross via the traffic lights to Lambeth North tube station (Bakerloo line, one stop to Waterloo).

www.ingramcontent.com/pod-product-compliance
Lightning Source LLC
Chambersburg PA
CBHW031423160426
43196CB00008B/1025